L I S T E N

ALSO BY STEVEN CRAMER

Clangings (2012)
Goodbye to the Orchard (2004)
Dialogue for the Left and Right Hand (1997)
The World Book (1992)
The Eye That Desires to Look Upward (1987)

LISTEN

Steven Cramer

MadHat Press
Cheshire, Massachusetts

MadHat Press
PO Box 422, Cheshire MA 01225

The Library of Congress has assigned
this edition a Control Number of
2020941376

ISBN 978-1-952335-08-2 (paperback)

Cover image: *The Deep* (1953) by Jackson Pollock
© 2019 The Pollock-Krasner Foundation / Artists Rights
Society (ARS), New York
Cover design by Marc Vincenz
Book design by MadHat Press

www.MadHat-Press.com

To Hilary, Charlotte, and Ethan

Contents

I.

II.

The main thing was being alive. That was the main thing.
    —Rilke, *The Notebooks of Malte Laurids Brigge*

I.

Bad

It got bad; pretty bad; then not
so bad; very bad; then back to bad.
Jesus, let's let things not get even worse.

A weird fall. Nearly ninety
one day, leaf mold making the house
all red eyes and throats. Don't think

about Thanksgiving, but hope
for a decent Halloween. Everywhere
gas-powered leaf-blowers growling—

Christ, let's let things not get even worse.

South Belknap

Jake says: "first time I recall wanting to die I was eight.
When I tried and nearly did I really wanted to live."

The room has gone around the room, first names
only, and favorite foods. Danielle said: "I hate food."

Lois says: "I know what happened happened only once.
I also know it's happening all the time." In jogging shorts,

his knees scabbed like an eight-year-old's, Seth says:
"I hope to radically accept distress from now on,

and maybe bear it skillfully?" Blue of two spruce trees,
the burnt-orange brickface of Admissions, summer green

of the lawns. Mark writes on the white board: "Men are not
disturbed by things, but by the view they take of them."

While most scribble this sentence into notebooks
on their laps, two or three look out the one window.

They see water from a fountain surge, plume, crest,
then fall into a pond no bigger than a toddler's pool,

and a boy with sinewy clots of hair, still as a page
in a picture book, bows to read his cell phone,

and sparrows fly into and out from the azaleas,
and roses flicker, fire from a magician's fingertips.

Zuni Fetishes, Santa Fe

Raven eats maize; Badger, ground turquoise;
Eagle, the guts of slain prey, but what
could feed this being dry as fossilized

dung? You took me in hand; we looked
at mesas, cottonwoods, arroyos; the Rio
Chama wound its umber cure our way.

Such medicines I spat back, and studied
instead the raptor's femur at Ghost Ranch,
my soul hollow as O'Keeffe's ram skull.

Under the crags of Echo Amphitheater,
I watched for the blood of the slaughtered
said to have entered the pores of the rock,

so our echoes echo their cries. And now
we're back: the night sky's sucked in its stars,
speed-limits shrink, we have to trace our snow-

prints to relieve the dog. What I love most
about you is your patience, the way you check
my climate while I shadow-box with silence.

But first, love, help me stop playing dead.

The World

Balancing on his haunches, snapping at a stuffed frog I dangle above his jaws, Zeus's front paws look puny as a kangaroo's. He can hold the position for an astonishing 8 to 10 seconds. If I were an honest parent, I'd explain to him the futility of changing one's nature—like trying to mate different species of butterflies. There he goes again, the little boxer ... and here I go again, remembering the June my rage overheated until it pounded music out of the stereo with a mallet. Everyone I loved stopped their horseplay. I saw two futures—one a moonlit shoreline; one a diagnosis. There was a third future I didn't see. Although I haven't yet used the word "world," when I do, I won't mean what that woman meant, index to her temple as she asked: *how do you bring the world into your thinking about art?* That whole summer my black razor-point pens, when laid side by side, looked like bodies in body bags.

A Cosmography of Melancholy

The three years I spent on Mars
mainly I felt bored.
Which is to say Mars might as well be Hell.
Next to boredom, shame's
the feeling most akin to a sweat-
heavy hair shirt previously owned by Satan.
With each new breath I took in the red ambiance,
Earth looked more like one of those trick paintings—
first a skull,
then a lady at her vanity,
then a skull again,
then a shaving mirror clouded with shower steam.
As a species we want *gravitas,* I thought,
and got more bored trying to remember
who invented prayer, which is to say
don't we all need some way to shut up
the troll within the troll within the troll?
Other than the Sea of Crises,
which anyway's a landmark on the Moon,
or the Plain of Judgment and the Vale of Mourning
and the Elm to Which False Dreams Cling,
which anyway are sites to see in Hades,
about my sojourn in the brutish atmosphere of Mars
there's nothing more to say—
other than, Do you know the mosquito
eater doesn't eat mosquitoes?
It drinks from the Sea of Nectar—then, when it's all
grown up, has sex and dies. Bitterly, bitterly.

Lackawanna

My brain felt swiped clean.
I couldn't love
songs I loved; friends came

nameless as mailmen …
A loaf of dough
forbidden to rise,

I'm slid into the hollow magnet.
Din of a dozen arcade games, but louder.
The MRI finds no sign

of stroke; the EEG, no fried circuitry.
Short-Term Temporal Lobe Seizure.
I'm told: forget it.

Forget my state of forgetfulness …
Was *Dismal Harmony* a childhood
wildlife preserve?—near tracks

where *Lackawanna* means
two streams meet and divide
in the tongue of an obliterated tribe.

Thought Experiment

Before my pupils gape *oh* in unison,
I find a seat with the semi-sighted

like myself, becalmed
in our separate intermissions
between medium to close-up shots

of cornea and lens,
and the deep blue look at fovea,
macula, and optic disk.

Everyone's aura ripples about them,

a sign some take for the spirit;
others, an ocular migraine.

With chained pens, new patients
chronicle their histories of floaters,
clots, hard stools and easy bleeding.

Squints; frowns; stalls over gaps
in the body's time line.
Now *that's* a look I know—

memory's written records
always a chore, always.

In my novel's last scene I can read
without tearing, a woman peers
up from her torts to see

her striped shirt losing its stripes.

Prepped for the MRI, she eyes
a fire extinguisher, maybe her final
take on red. Light through the blinds

gone mica-bright, she leaves me
in a quicklime of slowed time

where the mind gets scoochy as a boy
in a polyester suit and the noose
of a tightened tie. Soon as I could,

I'd shed mine to hide in private
horse operas I produced, starred in,

always the same end: myself
caught in the dirty deputy's sights

and shot ... dead? Come on.

The woman on my lap's a closed book.
What's meant when we say Mind
anymore—that's gone the way

the self went, let alone the soul.

Under my book light tonight,
a micro-surgeon's feather scalpel
cuts through upper gum and nasal bone—

the growth that bloats the gland
that pressures the optic nerve in its fold
of brain excised, so she's spared

losing sight of this blistering,
woeful, awfully worried planet.

I Want That

As I lay down too tired to believe
is a line I love by Laura Jensen.
I imagine it coming to her quickly
like dictation, like cold with snow.

I want that. How I want that.
And the night I believed I sat
in a chair in the middle of the sea
and yet could see the shoreline:

lights, dune grass, a hut, and bluffs
behind them bright, as if on fire—
Oh, I want them, I want them
back like the waterfall a child built

of cheesecloth, papier-mâché, wire.
I called it *Salishan,* a name sounding
like silver buffed up to a shine.
I want that shine too; a ton of it.

I brush my hand across rough cotton
here, or here. And notice, if I'm naked,
the pelt of shower water against my skin,
the scent of scentless soap, the weight

my feet confer to the tub floor. Today
I'll amble through the city's jazz of rain.
And the voice beneath my scalp that says
there's little to no point? Poor voice.

Written During a Depression

There once was a man with no imagination. He never even dreamed.

Neuroscientists claim that when you wake convinced you haven't dreamed, you've actually forgotten four to six excursions into a mailbox the size of a covered bridge, where a family of scorpions affix price tags to paperweights.

In this way, you're like the man—call him Man II—who forgets to tip his daughter for Thanksgiving dinner.

As for Man I, nothing: no keel-billed toucan on his shoulder when he looks in the mirror; no sonic puns on *fatigued* and *graffiti;* no grandmothers, in the guise of cats wearing Balinese masks, performing shadow dances to "Funeral March of a Marionette."

Man II, as a boy, had fantasies of eloping with a trapeze artist.

There she is now, swinging back and forth between Niagara and Victoria Falls. Just try calling *her* a dream.

After Tomaž Šalamun

Before I died, I could hear singing from under ash heaps.
Motor oil dripped a rosary on the blacktops.
I rose with vapor from August dew.
I dueled with oak branches.

I walked through my smoldering city, whistling.
Not one cloud, but you couldn't see the sun.
Keep going, I thought, *you can sleep under trestles and loot as
        you wish.*
Heat exhaled through cracks in the sidewalks.

Red ants stormed an apricot pit.
I stole an extra pair of socks off a dead man.
Birds behaved like birds—that is,
like the reptiles from which they're descended.

Flashlights burned white, then amber, then not at all.
I carried somebody's mother on my back.
We sank into mud up to my knees, my thighs, my waist,
while God called out, *Get over here, and right this minute.*

Three Versions of Mandelstam

1909

What should I do with this body?
I'm it and it's me. Who do I thank

for the quiet luck of breath, for being
alive: please tell me. I'm very good

at gardening and flowering. I'm
my own companion in the world's

solitary. Breathing on the window
of infinity, I can see a pattern

in the warm haze left on the glass,
a sign I hadn't recognized till now:

it condenses, gone; but the design
I love can't be effaced. That stays.

*

1933

We live numb to the homeland under our feet.
Get too close, our whispers disperse to mist.

But anywhere you stop to talk, the talk
gravitates toward the Kremlin mountaineer—

fingers fat as earthworms, his thumbs slugs;
his every word a gram, a pound, a ton.

Laughter wets his roach-brown upper lip;
it glitters spit-and-polish, like his boots.

His thuggish chicken-men encircle him.
One by one, as he dandles them, they croon

and simper, or miaow: Siberian cats.
But only he's allowed to bellow out

sentence after sentence, like horseshoes
flung at the groin, brain, forehead, eyes.

A firing squad floods his mouth with sweet
relish, his chest warm as a hug from home.

*

Voronezh, 1937
I'm still not dead, I have company
in a woman wearing the sort of rags I wear.
Across the tundra, bliss still reaches me
through fog, and squalling snow, and hunger.

My poverty's a miracle, what I lack
a type of wealth. Alone, heartened, at peace,
I kneel to the night and to the day. Work
that sings from a full throat must be blameless.

The sad man runs from snarling dogs
on a shadow's orders, into the wind's edge.

The poor man, waking from a coma, begs his shadow: *can you spare some change?*

Argumentum ad Lapidem
While on an Elliptical

Per usual this gym day, the world is all
that is the case, unless the opposite's true,
and nothing is. "I refute it *thus!*" confuted
Samuel Johnson, booting a rock to rebut
Bishop Berkeley's equally entrenched sense
that while the world's foot gets past the door
via eye, ear, nose, tongue and skin, that self-
same world's ultimately nil. Yet, neither
is it snagged in a world-wide web of dream—
wrap your mind around *that*

                    —or so he thought.
Who thought? I'm lost. I guess I meant
how Johnson's plea to a stone begot a new
iconic sound-bite certain to beguile his chum
and future profiler, Boswell, who loved him well,
as I do, especially for this diss: "be dull in a new way
and many will think you great." Love it. But

how slavishly I brandish quotes: *that* I dislike—
like playing dummy to your own ventriloquist;
like plagiarizing the smartest kid in the class;
like borrowing Diogenes's lamp, its sulfur
and lime wick aflame in secondhand bodhi;
like … now where *was* I?—

                       climbing
in place. Hearts run downhill in my family.
Systole, diastole—which is which? Who wrote what

verse, chorus, middle-eight, or lyric, John or Paul,
down to the minutest riff—those I have by heart;
also, who played which Frankenstein, Karloff
or Glenn Strange. And yes, I know it's wrong
to call the creature by its maker's moniker,
but after all, the name stuck, and isn't that
what we want?—

                to pass on some baton
of renown, however thin, to our offspring,
coterie, hamlet, city, nation; or if we're biggety,
the globe itself. And yet, what good's leaving
behind a humankind of groupies, if in life
you couldn't pick yourself out in a lineup?

"You think too much about thinking,"
says a friend. He likes the Pointillist's dots
of blue and yellow. I like the in-between
green they collaborate to make. We lost touch
around the time my mind became my *bête noire* …
Speaking of, for the first time in my sweat-stained
rumination, I've looked up. All four monitors
simulcast our unelected bully holding hands
with the-one-shaped-like-a-gelded-panda.
God help us, I think, but my thought misfires.
Can anyone tell wisdom from despair?

Costco

Jars of Heinz the size of Grecian urns;
enough Reynolds Wrap to foil an asteroid,

Eros in particular. Who's not aroused
by sales? My cart's heavy as the Fiat

I watched four Romans lift into a spot
downwind from the Coliseum's air

of cat piss. Sun through skylights
makes lap-tops, flat-screens, and vats

of Tide shine. Putti-like, kind of,
sparrows loft down from the vaults.

But when a day's gone oyster-gray,
its weight a ten-pound tub of putty,

all the wholesale sponges in the world
can't suck up this sense that I'm a poor

generic thing, reduced to *Creature
Double Feature*'s Incredible Shrinking

Everyman. His six-pack pre-steroid,
a three-cent stamp for his loincloth,

he dueled housecats with a safety pin,
giving heart to boys small for their age,

until he kept on shrinking to a voice-over
of cosmic dust, hack actor risen to the stars.

Listen

Can that really be Walt Whitman
on a wax cylinder chanting "America"—
Centre of equal daughters, equal sons...?

Sounds like he's gargling pebbles,
his larynx literally *form'd of this soil.*
In fact, he sounds like Uncle George,

the one man in my family to kill
Krauts in World War II and return
drunk again. Most mornings he nursed

the same German stein. So badly
did he stutter, you'd think he licked
all the alum off his styptic pencil ...

Some speculate that Edison recorded
Whitman's trebly voice—another thing
linking him to Lincoln—in West Orange,

town I visited nearly every weekend since
I adored my cousin Al, George's son.
Al's mother's name ... Aunt ... Aunt ...

I don't remember. I could phone Marti—
the other of two siblings out of four
left alive past sixty. Family genealogist,

she's traced Dad's line to Mary Chilton,
first woman ashore at Plymouth, entitling me
to Lowell's title, "Mayflower Screwball."

Why? Well, Marti found an 1830
Mendham census designating *lunatick*
as Nathan Cooper Cramer's occupation;

Dad chatted with his brother, Alfred,
dead since Anzio, in his shaving mirror;
and after ECT, TMS, and other acronyms

for stir-fried brains, McLean's in my phone.
How the hell did I get *here?* And what
sector of my face do I first touch

a razor to? The bedlam of thought
I have in mind is a sputter of dis-
sociation you, you only, can talk down.

No shock, then, after Whitman's high-wire
aria, real or forged; after my pickled uncle's
PTSD; after the father of the phonograph;

after my Pilgrim forebear who became
an orphan six weeks after touching land,
it's you I'll be listening to at the last. How

resonant—the bones of our middle ears.

II.

Self-Portrait with Insomnia, Rocks, and Fireflies

I might have been encoded
a few eons ago
as an oblong stone, flat and perfect for skipping,
kissed and kissed and kissed; and if pitched
skillfully enough, Mystic Lake
wets me a fourth time,
then settles me bottomward,
one among millions
cast into the snail's pace of underwater time.

But it's Wednesday, Love,
well past midnight. I've been peering
into the jolt of a black window.
I could swear I see the fireflies
that teased a summer lawn
decades ago, the flash-black-flash of their belly-lamps.

They're beetles, not flies—
did you know that?
                    Neither did I.
A sort of enzyme—Luciferin—combines
with oxygen to create their light.
Nobody knows what makes the light
switch on and off, least of all
the darning needle of my wakefulness
practicing its stalls over a lake
that might have *bitten* or *licked* as readily as *kissed.*

And besides, what I'm calling fireflies
we called lightning bugs. None of us
connected their glow with sex,
and beside you now I'd swear to anything:
I'm *that* tired in this sleepless daydream
as a deeply appreciated pebble, while a ring
of rocks circles the August lakefront fire—

on each rock, someone chants,
but we chant the most persuasive chant
up from the bottom of the lake.
Hearing that chant, the shell-
halves of their hands keeping time,
everyone thrust into future and past
listens and regrets a little less.

A Habit

If she's unhappy, she stays upstairs.
For him, less time spent alone the better.
Sometimes, though, he'll linger in his parked car
until the engine cools. If it's raining …

The day they met, he tells new friends,
a busker played Beatles on a glass harmonica.
Memory's more like lightning bugs, she thinks—
you need to see them twice to track them.
She keeps a notebook for ideas like this.

Married nearly thirty years, for a time
they discussed retiring near the ocean—
Gloucester, perhaps, or maybe Rockport.
All those years and not one affair, a fact
they're proud of, but try not to belabor

… unlike their one son,
about whom they'll talk relentlessly.
Watching the child sleep through turbulence,
he stopped white-knuckling and she started.

Three or four dark periods.
They've learned to keep an argument
from withering into rage, a process
of retreat, or so it seems to her.

In their wedding video, more couples
no longer couples, and many ghosts.
That's him, of course. That's how he thinks.
Now, after sex, they press their palms, hard,
against each other's ears—inducing
for that moment before they disengage
the feeling of being both deafening and deaf.

Note to My First Wife

We leased a two-story coloring book.
The peonies our neighbor planted

between our *recto* and her *verso*
turned out plastic to the touch.

She even kept them watered: pretty
funny, like the niblets we bought

in white cans named NO NAME.
But it's the moon who found us

really hilarious that night—naked,
well-oiled from head to foot—

we swam across Lake MacBride.
No memories of you in snow …

I assume you sleep as I do, more
or less. When I can't, can't you?

Ginkgo trees canopied our one-
way street, no address to GPS.

Stopped for geese at Fresh Pond,
or the news on mute, I hear you,

also turned down low, say *don't
bother wondering if I'm dead.* I do.

Without a Name for This

Quiet as whispered scripture, certain names
freeze on our tongues whenever we say them.
Who's the one who called me a misfortune,
slamming the phone down? Who's the one
who rose up before me, who made me feel
my whole body breathing, not just my lungs?
Who's that dancer limbering up in the museum,
at home in the edgy white light as we stare?

Now I'm left rummaging through the house,
and its many swollen drawers, for a picture
of her, her, her, timelessly holding my hand
before the reversal, before my atlas to the past
lost its binding, pages scattering. As little as a whiff
of clove reminds me of so much leaving, though
it doesn't matter who's to blame. No one is.

It's time I stopped standing before my own lens,
my face like a thumb print on the glass. Time
to stop expecting the secret to arrive simply
by shutting my eyes and holding still. Years ago,
I thought all I needed was a guide to songbirds,
the tanager's *keep back keep back* and all that.
How do you learn to look to yourself like a child,
with understanding and bewilderment at once?

The Great Chain of Being

A Renaissance courtier serenades his lady, her porcelain flesh
massed above a stomacher, his Venetian breeches expansive
as Philip Sidney on the virtues of artifice. What else can be
guessed about the lady's figure rhymes with the shape of her
gentleman's mandolin. She sits on a mossy knoll; his smile is
Latinate.

The spirals of their matching ringlets;
his velvet pumps pinked with tiny holes;
her delicate pinsons—or are they pincnets?
the two trees branching over them, which touch to make
       an arch, like a couple dancing the Allemande, a
       metaphor for the rational Universe.

If you want visual proof of their place on the Great Chain of
Being, you'll find them in an attic I'm not sure exists anymore.
You'll have to climb stairs steep as a ladder, and rummage
through dusty boxes for the remains of the china set, *circa*
1950s or '60s, on which they'll still be courting. Between each
chipped and washed-out piece: a sheet from the *Times* or the
Star Ledger. Even after half a century, a headline like *Man
Walks on Moon* may still come as a shock.

In Favor of Magical Thinking

They're in from the cold, look!—men dressed
as ladies, ladies as adjutants general. Inside
each warlock or witch, a child. The servants
wipe frost from their masks and false beards.

Nickolai and Sonya, his "gorgeous hussar,"
steal away, under ice-burdened poplars,
to the barn. Listen: whisper of pouring grain
in an empty loft says you'll marry; silence—

you'll marry for money. In the back pantry,
the maid drips molten wax into water, sees
war in the hardening figures. Let the snow be
not just eternal but immortal for our couple.

Forget the future's cocked pistol to the head.
Breathe in the scent of burnt cork from her lips.

The Game

Let me clarify some things about the game.
First rule: think about the game, you've lost.
No tiles, cards, currency, whirling dials: all pieces

are included, space has been cleared at the table.
Join in. Your turn. Kids learn the game in school
corridors, score it in red along their forearms,

new slices on old. It doesn't end when the day ends:
race for the stairs, dodging the geeks and slow kids,
thunder of fists on lockers, last push to the streets.

The old hands they become play all night, by daylight
a winner still in doubt. *Friction Ridge, Lake of Enclosure,*
Dot and Spur: its variants can wear a pencil to its nub.

Wedded to the game, couples bop to the *Heart-Flip,*
the *Mind-Winder,* later to lie on sheets deliberately
left blank. Who invented the game? Who made up

the jokes passed from laugh to laugh? Black suit
for weddings, same for the funeral. In between, quick
as a nail sparks an Ohio Blue Tip, it fixes in its sights

the boy who puffs, walks; leaves in a down of frost
crushed beneath his feet. At the ridge he'll climb,
sun warms the girl expecting him, curve of her hand

moist to take him. When he comes, the game beats
in his heartbeat thumped by the wallop of her heart
beating against his; and like a spider tumor, spins

webs in his brain, in love now with how it's played.

Chthonic

Timed for odd noons, eight sprinklers mist
ten minutes each; a ninth soaks the hedge
row of yews: each May, a new price hike
just to siphon up my underworld river.

No coin for the ferryman, it's a pauper's
gate to hell … In the den, three tweens,
one mine, pass from hand to hand their lip-
gloss foraged from the mall. Graces now,

but in a wink, gray ones trading a single eye …
They're pre-hormonal, prideful, venereal
nouns, fountainheads of argot pumped
to flow disdain. About their future boys

in the vestibule, shuffling their hooves,
all trident-quick moves once in the car—
think too much, thought's a venomed pelt.
It's exquisite, yes, to touch a spider web

to gold, but bread and water's better.
Whoever thought it wise storing hope
at the bottom of a jug, thought best.
Let it steep, sweet as the devil's-food

and Capri Sun these girls bid me bring.
Inside them, thirst and hunger pulse
like p.s.i.'s channeling through pipes.
Autumn and winter: frozen Mars Bars

and Log Cabin syrup dripped on snow.
Spring: stained eggs on a fake green bed.
Summer: the earth and earth's daughter,
by August the girl's step heavy, tugged at.

She's moistening her lips for Hades' kiss.

Calling Back

My daughter sings in snow falling through the scent of red oak or ash, some flakes large enough to contain passages from Emily Dickinson's letters. I'm not close enough to identify the texts. Just a few nouns or verbs—*dew, fan, plash, honors*—tongue touching on the teeth to sound the dentals, teeth on the bottom lip to form the fricatives, both lips pouting the plosives, the vowels vibrating in the cave of the mouth. If I were Dickinson, my daughter's song might toll like a shipwrecked church bell; the gist of it, sudden as a bird rowing in, then swallowed by, the firmament. The snowing sky has just gone whiter. Twenty, maybe twenty-five years left, unpolished stones in a glass.

The Glen

Beginning with a phrase from Stevens's letters

1

After too much midnight, it's pleasant to hear the milkman—
a pleasure, too, to recall the milk left on the doorstep,
especially in winter, stems of cream thrust past the bottle-
necks capped with gold foil. Before long, though, Mother's

back from the married widowhood she lived through
in a neighborhood bordering the woods bordering the glen:
valley-glade where kids probed and necked and stripped.
Father's elsewhere; and was, it must be said, an awfully

handsome man. Ex-track star. Might have modeled; wore
black or gray windowpane suits, topped with a fedora
Mother smiled at. Hating her teeth, she never grinned.
There's her sepia smile from my wall. Nowhere near,

Father sank two holes in one. In one lifetime. Not bad.
Nearly godly-looking, he made it his right to take women.
That's him stealing up the walk, past midnight, Oxford
lace-ups printing the moonlit snow, pink El Dorado

ticking itself to sleep in the garage, Mother's Olds beside it
cold. And his scent—Cutty Sark, Kents—slips into bed.
Look, say the neighbor's windows, *she has four children; where's
the husband?* Snow fills his footsteps, whiting out the gossip.

2

Every few years, the shade of it comes back: the black
our hands got, crushing walnut leaves, deep blue beads,
thousands, in the streambed. No one knew where from.
Once, a neighbor girl, squatting to pee, astonished me

with the brow of stubble above her … who knew what,
at ten, to call it? Older kids fingered, sucked, and under
the glen's oak crowns, I first heard sex misunderstood:
"it's what whores do for money," Mark alleged,

his grin wide with misinformation. So "what's
a whore?" was the question I put to Mother,
not Father, and fetched her scotch. Her story
of the body, indelible as blue dye, left its stain.

3

The morning I caught Mother showering,
if she saw me, she didn't scold; but the shame
of her hair I stared at, raw as skin scrubbed
to a blush, still scalds my eyes. Forty years

Father lived to rut. Mother stewed, kept mum
as their plaster statuette on our hearth, *Two Gents*—
Dickensian sideburns, spatterdashes, pleats, vests.
Listen, whispers one, while the listener grins.

Every Three Years

a death. He'd watch them go
like people strolling, in pairs or alone, beside a canal,
before rounding the bend of the towpath.

Some, after passing from sight, found cities or farms.
Some vanished in the heat-haze of an August afternoon,
or in November fog that thickens near waterways.

Sometimes his wife asleep beside him seems to be three—
one who says, *see them making pig-noses at the window?*
another who says, *you'll see them soon enough;*

and one who says—
but right now he can't recall the third thing she says,
the thing, every day, he counts on her to say,

as she had yesterday, but had she the day before?—
each day behind the next, like rows of hay bales across a field
that slopes into another field, with more rows of bales ...

Other times, he's reading to his dead from a picture book,
holding up the illustrations, panning them from left to right,
pausing at each face, so everyone can see.

Flight

We're in bad, we're in terrible, shape
when it comes to time. Like a clock-
face not so much a circus ring of hours

as Dali's melting watch; like the boy
with senioritis, who says "who cares?
it's just history," and grows to a man

never missing a reunion; like Sungir
mammoth hunters, who glue 60 fox
incisors to the belts of their dead,

their *important* dead, for the trek home;
like early filmmakers, who understood
and then, but hadn't mastered *meanwhile;*

like the wedding VHS moved to DVD,
then to the Library in the Cloud, seen
years later, divorce exceeding marriage,

then replayed another decade on,
divorce outstripped by the dead;
like headstones with a birth and death

date, plus one birth date and a dash—
the widows having lots of friends to do
stuff with, no one to do nothing with;

like … *Enough!* or *Too Much!* Slow *down.*
Common swifts are so adapted to flight
they don't, or almost don't, have legs.

Elegy to My Family

My middle name went down in the Tyrrhenian
off Anzio Beach, life jacket filling with the sea.

After that, my father, split in half, would sing
into the bathroom mirror, where his twin lived.

After she died, we found poems my mother wrote
to her five dogs, each killed by a neighbor's car.

You do what you have to do was a motto she loved
saying over and over. Her tailor's dummy,

buxom amputee, lived in the attic. The attic,
said Bachelard, denotes the rational mind,

but the basement's where I find my brother,
back from the hungry i, strumming his Martin D-18.

He came of age in the era of the pocket radio,
The Kingston Trio, and public swimming pools

that polio closed. Era when the sky might catch fire.
To improve us, my aunt read uncensored Grimm—

Rumpelstiltskin danced until he tore himself in two.
She'd write to Richard Tucker, and he wrote back

twice, and sang Verdi from a boom box in hospice.
In a dream I hold my sister's hand. A walk, yes,

a walk would be good. New moon. Poplars circle
the duck pond. New Jersey church spires blacker

than the black sky. What I tell her wakes me up.

III.

American Freedom

The poet gets a call from *American Freedom.*
He doesn't pick up. He'd been reading a thriller
in which the timing device requires a code
spelled B-A-B-Y. Punch it in, you survive.

He writes an email quoting Naomi Klein—
"for the men who rule this world, rules
are for other people"—stashes it in *Drafts*
to save for second thoughts. So what's

running the gamut in the poet's memory?
A neighbor he saw spurt out his front door,
his face gone redder than the bloodier
verses in the Bible; then a man he watched

pray to a singing bowl struck with a mallet,
tones so lovely he considered praying too.
When the obits of seventeen students grin
from *The Times* and *The Globe,* for a day or two

poetry feels shifty, a stump speech. "Never
write a poem about anything that needs a poem
about it," wrote Richard Hugo. Dick, he thinks,
times change. Meanwhile, the hawthorn

in his yard extends its scabby limbs, thick
as Doric columns, over Bedford's thoroughfare
to and from school. For the sake of the kids
who scuffle by, it's got to be cut down.

Sketches at the Hayden Rec Center

A solitary clock behind bars, floors
forbidden to street shoes, exit signs—

one, two, three, four: fine—and waxy cries
of boys, one mine, practicing their dribbling

and bank shots. My eyes closed, the volley
of Spaldings pounds like opening night

of Operation Desert Storm, or Shield, or
whatever war our Sonys dust up next ...

Opening my eyes, I glimpse, time-lapse,
the pierced, lovely lips and eyebrows

of the future for these boys. Give them,
please, their share of nitrogen, oxygen,

and the less-than-one-percent of "other"
my son and I idled in, *en route* to Hayden,

in line at Walgreen's new drive-through,
watching a man cradle tulips to his van.

To study electricity, you need lights,
a Baghdad schoolteacher said on NPR—

after which we learned the hawk sees
eight times better than us. What gives

deadly eyesight to that beauty of a bird,
what gave those tulips an edgy splash

of apricot against the parking lot's
fresh tarmac and knolls of sod—is that

what can't simmer down inside these boys?
Oh, they're trying, as the coach requires,

to stretch their fingers, rotate their necks.
When his whistle fires them down-court,

into the 30-second zone, they're home—
targeting each other, being themselves

targeted. At my son's age, I drilled
my blue and gray sharpshooters, and had

by heart the total killed and wounded
at Bull Run ... A few more chest-shots

and time's up. I peel my son off the pine
handholds bolted to cinder-block walls;

navigate him toward the snack machine
for cheddar fries and Sprite; then to the car

where, sliding him into the back, I get
this burst of scent: part cheese-product,

part lemon-lime and sweat-tang in his hair;
and from the drugstore lot across the street

where a man hugged color like a pass
completed, the mix of damp earth and tar.

Born to Be Wild

Zeus keeps watch at the window,
jumpy as a rookie air traffic controller,
growling at the moon. Or is he mourning
our kids grown up and gone? Don't know—
the way I can't recall whose piss drooled down
my back in a Brookside, New Jersey dugout,
since 1968 was such a good year for thugs.
Okay, we were too coddled to be thugs as such.
Racoons subsisted on the backyard trash
of our Humphrey moms and Nixon dads—
the miracle of eight-track in their Cadillacs
that chauffeured us to dances we didn't dance.
Ken, Tom, Fred, and I preferred to be the band,
since bands stood taller by virtue of standing
on wobbly lunchroom tables we made a stage.
Bands might play "Born to Be Wild" six times
a night and still not have the song by heart.
This was before the G-clefs of millennial sex
tattooed the torsos and butts of our young.
Still, we were melancholy as birthday cakes,
rose from our beds like mist off a duck pond,
our eyes more like lab rats' the farther back
we smoked what we called dope on the bus.
Dumb as lint, we thought we looked straight
into history, but history was—as history is—
lying in wait like a riptide or an undertow.
So much of our lives we live over our heads!
And thus, fast-forward to this childless night

from which I'm glancing back, making shit up
to a photo of my kids, backs turned, facing the sea.

Independence Day

Hammer-strokes of unmediated rage—

two men face off; one is waving
his weeping wife and son into a van

half in, half out, of its parking space;
the other's bike, wheels revolving,

lies upended on the sleek asphalt;
flanking him, two girls; everyone's

okay. Sunday, dew-point record high,
a hate-group has a permit to collect,

first, outside the Unitarian church, then
to protest gay wedlock on the Green,

where every Independence Day
middle-aged merchants and retirees

in breeches and tricorn hats
shoot muskets and pretend to kill

or die. "You're asking *me* to pay
for a scratch on your bumper? Look

at my daughters!" They've straggled
back to their banana seats and tasseled

handlebars. Their flushed cheeks
glisten in the heat. With her thumb,

one pumps her bike's bell-trigger. It
clicks; doesn't ring. Her sister twists

a braid. *To Combat Hate; Ignore It*—
our police chief opined in his Op Ed ...

"You'll pay, all right, or I'll call the police!"
My son's hand tightens in my hand.

"Did the van hit the bike or the bike
the van?" asks one of the assembled

to no one in particular, as the man—
which man?—flips open a cell phone:

"Somebody, please, be my witness."

Dorado

Royal palms all over; men shimmy up
the trunks, machetes clenched in their grins;
coconuts thud like dud bombs on the lawn …

At the edge of this U.S. protectorate,
sun mutes the Coquí frogs, whose choruses
of night-chirps named them. By "the world's

longest river pool," hibiscus widen
red yawns; spider lilies and heliconia
mass in plots, their brass plaques, stolid

as palace guards, list phylum and class.
Our Hyatt has evolved a new wing:
time-share suites teem with gringos

like us. The old crescent Cerromar,
closed except for the casino—its dreamed
future more yanks buying time—sits stalled

in litigation. Potted shield-ferns
block unlit corridors, elevator doors
jammed in gap-toothed quiet. From Celia,

orchestrating poolside shuffleboard,
or from Diego, the Bohio's quick-draw
bartender (so many years alert to thirst

his hair's gone gray along with ours)—
we hear their every *gracias* imply: *amigo,
let us be the last resort of your empire.*

But how one power ends, the next begins—
that's beyond us all. Halfway around the world,
in Beijing, thousands labor sunup to sundown

to fill our Banana Republics. A few yuan
skim the first off a pallet of beach shirts,
then I'll pay eighty dollars for the last,

unbuttoning its silk off the manikin.
His pecs a brazen gold in the shop-glass,
he knows another *Medium*'s on its way

to cover him. Capital: no more chance
to tame it than to rid the Swan Café
of *chongas*—those aboriginal crows

Julio curses and fans three menus at.
Each year they thicken on the netting,
peck a new hole in, raid unbussed tables,

crap on the plates, beguile then terrify
the younger kids. There's one now, and look:
another's battling a third over some fries.

Sunday Morning

In one version of the future, only expert burrowers survived. Their children learn quickly, scrabbling through the tunnels their parents left them in; squaring the support beams, adding pit stops at fallout shelters; bypasses around sequoia roots; unsettling structures with exotic names like Zanzarière; making the abandoned roadbeds on the surface quake. A recently unearthed blueprint shows a network vexing as a subway map of Manhattan. At last report, moles, earthworms, and prisoners of war have put aside their differences and begun to organize.

Memo to self: *burrowers* or *borrowers?* Self to memo: silence.

Silent too is the creek that runs through the plot of suburban wilderness I see from my window, flanked by two scraps of spring snow. The swing set my kids hardly used, with its splintered ladder and listing slide: why haven't I taken it down? Or not silent, merely quiet; centuries have passed since any spot on the earth held its tongue.

Frontier

It wasn't easy to cross the border, but we did it
by forming groups of four, one person for each corner
of the earth, and moving through the dark suburbs
all winter. And afterward, our lives came to depend

on our myth, like the tales of Scheherazade. So many of us!
You couldn't leave your house without finding clusters
of us bundled together like evicted families, some
with dogs trotting behind, some with umbrellas,

some casting shadows twice their size on the painted
backdrops to our journey. And we knew we'd be freed
when we arrived—that much the legends verified—
every parched lip and blistered tongue would have its say

and once the testimony ended, the trials would end
in acquittal, the sirens would cease, and we'd be able to sleep.
How can you say, after all our efforts, that we were wrong?
That the other side of the frontier beckoned with a lie?

A Burn So Bad It Requires Ice

Sometimes I believe people with substance
abuse issues have all the fun. After all,
it's the ovaries and liver of the scrumptious

pufferfish that literally take your breath away.
Today, during K. 183, back comes Mozart's
metaphor for passion I just made up: *a burn*

so bad it requires ice. For years, in my fridge,
I kept my cocaine in glass vials the size
of Lilliputian beer mugs—where did you

keep yours?—and entered the era's debate
about which end of an egg a loyal citizen
cracks first. I loved many things I didn't

understand: modern sculpture, fondue,
that duct tape works least well on ducts,
that beauty like *abattoir* means *slaughterhouse.*

Now there's a carrot ruining history, don't
we need more words whose melodies can't
mean their meanings—*pulchritude,* for one?

I'll never ride that lofty Appaloosa …
For years I thought *scherzo* meant *schizo.*
For years priests turned cinctures into nooses.

So much about living is sadly mistaken.
So much of living should be titled "Untitled."
(For years priests turned cinctures into nooses.)

Some nights I go to my threadbare backyard,
stand there, quiet as a sun dial, staring at the sky,
and soon enough realize I'm looking at the stars.

Time Out

Said to know things about the soul we didn't,
the yogini told us to relax our anuses and sit;

and to let the shenanigans of our thinking
simmer down, which made me think of carting

toddler Charlotte and toddler Ethan, spraying clots
of teary snot, into their rooms for a Time Out,

all the while *don't hit don't hit* on replay. Then
she gave us this half-sentence to complete:

I feel in touch with others when … Which is when
a truck chirped the beep trucks make backing up

on this first open-window day in a bitter April,
which history shows *is* a cruel month. Who knew?

Lincoln shot, Hitler born, Titanic, Bay of Pigs,
King shot, Waco, the start of the Armenian

and Rwandan Genocides, Columbine, Virginia
Tech—yup, all April. You'd face as many horrors

googling May: most memes amount to lies.
Truth is, I lie more than I know, but I know it

took me less than a second to finish her phrase
in my head: *I feel in touch with others when afraid*

my kids will die before me. Some shared. Not me.
The exercise done, we filed out, anuses at peace.

Later, at the gym, the crazed babe of my fear
awoke, its arms and feet thrashing in a tantrum

I tried to quell by stretching: the gorilla stretch,
the cat-cow stretch, then back to the gorilla. Still,

fear hugged my knees so hard it brought me
close to kneeling. But I didn't, because I don't.

In Dunedin

Around the Octagon, people drink flat whites,
don't leave tips. Kiwis pay a living wage.
As overseas as the jet-lagged get—winter
in August; today yesterday in the States—
we sit like silhouettes, here and not here.

Lifting her white shift,
she pisses in a store-front, perineum
aimed at the café. In the book on my lap,
Leonardo's *Vitruvian Man,* his ideal body
squaring the circle; on our list of sights
not to be missed, blue penguins
waddling up-shore to nest.

Circling the square, her awful squawk
grows distant; comes back. She raises
her shift right at us. Hard to admit
our disgust reflex rises, like reflux;
harder still that she makes us feel
at home.

Charity

Every time the Pope shooed the beggar from the entrance to the Sacré-Cœur, she slid back into place seconds later, because who is a pope to judge? Even when he kicked her, dragged her away by her shawl, back she came, reliable as two sparrows playing tug of war with the heel of a baguette.

The one I call the Pope, I admit, was really a doorkeeper who aspired to be pope—who, ever since he was a boy, played Infallible with his mates and wore an ecclesiastical-looking collar and red running shoes.

The holier, more golden chambers of the church were under repair and off-limits. Tiers of lit votive candles. Hard to suppress an urge to give them cocktail umbrellas. They shivered like crowds massed before the ticket office for the Catacombs, where kilometers of skulls, humeri, and femurs are stacked in cords, half the skulls turned toward you, half turned away.

Ours

Sanibel Beach Resort

Years ago, we took us and our kids
on a 90-percent white cruise to Istanbul
from Rome. In no time I got smart
at discriminating my white from the others'.
I watched Italians bully in line for ice
tea or lemonade, the two free drinks—
their Dantesque vowels, honey on the page,
a sort of noise pollution in my airspace.
The English, being Brits, queued; the French
seemed to take their cues from the Italians.
The Germans had no sense of line at all.
But oh, my Americans, you made mouth-
sounds like rusted gears, belched at will,
your slurry banter fit for jotting down
only on the blackest cocktail napkins;
and not just did I know your every slight
(for an exhaustively ugly list, click here),
but by 'tween-age, I'd had the lot by heart.

Now, down in Sanibel, our Black
30-something waitress warms my coffee.
Our—no, *the*—server's Floridian lilt
has me constantly asking *sorry*—my tip,
at 18 percent, a runt of a reparation.
It's her kids, not ours, who will sink
first under the next flood. There's jack
shit that she, or semi-snow-birds like
ourselves, can do to stop it. "Is there

a map of downtown?" is the best
I've got to ask her; "what downtown?"
her best answer. What's in my head
is more or less in hers: gates that open
into gardens outside time. But each gate
locks out *them, us* in, our garden's *ours.*
She's about to clear away the yolky orts
of our *Americans.* We rise to go,
no clearer where, in America, we are.

The Look

I'll never tell Ethan I listen to him sing
in the shower. It might make him stop.
I like whoever's singing to keep singing.
I pause at the door until the water shuts.

To some, singing's a sin, a capital crime.
Some, to brighten their afterlives, pack
mirror shards into a pipe, thus boosting
their radius of kills, in song, at prayer.

Have you ever tried talking to a guitarist
as they play? Not on stage, of course,
but in a room where their strumming
consorts with the gossip. There's a look

I'll call *The Look.* My brother (1945–1990),
had it; my nephew—who, for a living,
bivouacs north of the Muir Woods,
making fire with a spindle, hearth-board,

bow, and bearing block—has it too:
a stare aimed through you, blank as sheets
of still-reamed paper, so anything you say
leaves no mark; a mindful mindlessness

where the work of play gets done. Ethan
grudgingly began on a Yamaha acoustic—
cheapest guitar you can buy that's not a toy—
thirty daily minutes of fretfully gripped chords.

Feeling his parents' mute cheerleading
from the living room—we feigned reading—
he retreated to the basement from the den.
We eavesdropped through the cellar door.

"English speakers know that *cellar door*
is among the loveliest phrases in our tongue,
especially if detached from its sense,"
said Tolkien—not the first to say it, but

"I have a hatred of apartheid in my bones"
belongs to him alone. Ethan's milestone
was a trademark lick: "House of the Rising Sun."
Work made play? Not quite. Songs still groped

to a halt. Dad to the marrow, I've hyped
his steps from chords to chord progressions
aspiring up the stairs. The ones he coined
he called *noodlings*—tunes stitched from bits

his hand happened on. Three years plus
our language blown to atoms: *losers, fake,*
haters, failing, fire and fury, and those two
so barefaced they spit: *excuse me; believe me …*

When Ethan finally added his own lyrics,
when what he wrote he sang, we listened
even closer through the cellar door—not
to a novice, but to a master, of the look.

IV.

An Invitation

Look through this hole in a stone wall
at the man in his bloated overcoat;
morning suit beneath it; around his neck
a thing half scarf, half boa constrictor.
He strides past alleyways brilliant
with yellow, orange, and green fruit rinds,
brownstones guarded by their ironwork
reflecting on the river. How he loves
these lovely things, and everything else:
sycamores amused by the tappling water,
come-hither, womanly shapes of churches.
He'd have loved to meet the architects!
When it rains he stays inside, but the sky
always burns blue, so he's always walking.
Everybody walking pleases him; and since
everybody's strange—aren't they?—strangers
in particular. No one's unsafe, except inside
everyone there's a kind of corroded iron
nobody not living in the moment sees.
When a woman out of Periclean Athens
nakedly appears in her first-floor window,
her ideal smile fills a gap in the nothing
he relives of his life. Moved in, he buys her
a bathrobe. Who's got a right to call him
selfish? He has what he wants, happily
ever after no less an invitation to ruin.
From now on he'll be longing for longing.

Drink

Drunk, I read a story about a drunk.
A meadow in the story, and birds singing,
give the man the shakes. He starts lying
on the couch his father passed out on,
staring at the painting of a meadow
his mother ripped from an art book.
The artist had a knack for daffodils, so
his wife made arrangements of narcissus
(from the Latin for *numbness* or *stupor*)
till trumpets blared at him from every nook.
By then he'd painted the wife next door.
"I've made it," he thought, "I'm all serenity,"
and began the work of his Sober Period.
In those days I was a high school student.
Even during gym, my best friend drank—
"To get ripped means you're working
on your six-pack," he broadcast to anyone.
His mother "felt a chill," "took to bed
with a brandy," before she disappeared.
You could say she'd been a meadow once.
Does amber bourbon in a Technicolor
'50s movie thrill you the way it thrills me?
In '30s black-and-white, rye looks like tea.
A moralist famous for condemning drink
once spoke in a speakeasy, with such fire
he lit a book of matches with his breath.
His fiancée, who worshipped him, burst in.
"You're drunk," she snarled, a comment
on the obvious that brought a smile even

to *her* lips. Tough smile to forget. "She ran into the street" is how this story ends, rain performing a pizzicato on the tree limbs and smacking her face. Out of the night a doorway appears into which she vanishes. Leave her there. Let's drink to her health.

The Benevolence of the Butcher

He's not history yet. He's as proud
of his work as a blood-spatter expert

breaking the code of sprayed gore.
Next door left, in the gourmet shop,

brie and baguettes; Love-Lies-Bleeding
in the garden center next door right.

Two witches, catty-corner, run
a crystal shop. Self is the artful

lies it tells itself, Mind is no more
than neural chuck. We know

it's only human to wait in line
for the choicest cuts, to forecast

when our number's up, to tense
what feels a lifetime for the shutter—

all that forbearance just to end up
a rat-eyed stiff. Blood-gouted

apron in a hamper, the butcher
drives home by instinct. At red

stoplights he clicks the seconds past
with his tongue, our supplest muscle.

Sewage Has Its Say

Give me roots prying into the joints
of your main waste line, Charmin
thickening her web first to a nest,
then to a dam—I sluice in reverse,

top the basement tub and spill
into a poem! Damn! I've sunken
to new heights! Will you take
a hint and stomach your disgust?

What does *The Thinker* look like
he's doing? How come Luther heard
God's thunderclap of justice via faith
whilst sitting on the privy? You know

where love's pitched his mansion, so
don't shower so much. Squeaky clean's
for mice. No soap's got enough tallow
to wash out the mouth mouthing off.

What made you so … *nice?* Polite's
kind of like death, isn't it? Okay, not
quite. But consider this, my sweet kin
in excretion: to flies we taste like candy.

Orphic

The sun gave birth to a rock that told
the truth. Some say it prowled down

from the hills, its surface too hard to score,
even with knives they fired and honed.

The clefts and rifts looked like wrinkles.
They chanted *wise, wise rock,* bathing it

in a spring, drying it with fresh linen.
They knelt before it, sang, and asked

if a god lived inside. It remained
rock—out of sullenness, some say.

To keep the peace, the elders agreed
to pass it from house to house, each

granted a day's audience, in private.
Some greeted it with scented oil lamps;

others just kept their porches swept.
Once indoors, some say, the rock spoke,

yet no one told what they heard—this rock
they spoiled, as mothers spoil their sons.

En Route

The church grew out of its mountain,
shone, baroque, in the sun—
stucco the color of bread crust.
The river foamed. For a moment,
one cloud passed over the water,
our table, not set,
strewn with leaves and ginger.

Where did he come from?—
the swimmer who surfaced
into our atmosphere of gnats.
No one expected he'd question us—
what brought us here and why—much less
that he'd point to the bridge up ahead.
To cross it, he said, you need a coin.

Then he pushed back into being
part of the current,
while somebody's small dog
started to yelp and strain
against his leash, as if he wished
to run with the river as far as he could.
His was the one familial voice in the heat.

Devotion Street

We needed and used each other, living
north of civilization, where we assumed
we'd been "delivered" over the transom
and into our rent-controlled brownstone.
We learned to love the word *apartment.*

Back from his spell among monks
packing hand guns under their cowls,
our novelist hardly ever left his desk,
typed *rat-at-tat* from dawn to midnight
like a raccoon scratching in the attic.

Our kick-boxing painter lent our bodies
muscles they hadn't earned. How easily
we'd strip for her, naked as pumice stone.
Our resident muse, a long-maned miracle,
made the Ouija's plastic planchette chat.

Or did she cheat, nudging it on the sly
to spell out fates she reckoned we deserved?
Our poet-memoirist worked hard to live
by "the double lullaby of the wide road,"
a line he wished he'd written, as do I.

Were we planets in the "goldilocks zone?"
No. Memory romances. We had our inner
juries—or is it furies?—who judged everyone.
Mine still hand down piercing, mousey verdicts,
as if they'd sucked in balloon-grade helium.

Turbulent, benign, like most heart murmurs,
we knew the syllabi we chose called for risk,
so we seriously played our fox-kit games.
I can't say I miss us anymore; can't say it
because it's true, I do. Now we conform

to other house rules, live in larger units,
and practice disparate ways to recognize
the minute-by-minute that comes rent-free,
though I still glance over my shoulder
to see who might be reading my last line.

The Question

Once there was a question so compelling
anyone who asked it, or had it asked of them,
was brought, willing or not, to their senses—

all of them at once. An apple bitten into,
the gritty taste and smell when waves withdraw—
pleasures like these cut to the brain like a stroke.

Most kept indoors, curtains drawn, and aged
into an oval of frowns around an oblong table,
sniffing, bemused, at their Salad Niçoise.

What to make of the single empty setting—
salad, napkin, and silverware untouched?
Well-read, you might think: *Macbeth*—

a brain so heat-oppressed it sees a dagger,
not yet bloodied, in the air. The light grows
dull, a chill leaks from the murky heath.

In years to come the question, always the question,
makes authors dump their laptops, directors
celebrated as the finest of their generation

quit their sets, painters slash their canvases,
and assistant professors relapse into undergrads
grieving their grades. Millennia ago, before

the question had a mind to think it up,
before Freud argued every dream's a wish …
whatever happened to that myth, I wonder?

Today teams of neuroscientists light up
sectors of the brain where empathy resides.
"Resides" isn't right, of course, and yet

these regions also govern our heart rate—
a nice slant that doesn't change the fact
we hate waiting for even the smallest reward.

Mentalese

The idea that thought is the same thing as language is an
example of what can be called a conventional absurdity.
—Steven Pinker

The apology I woke from
left guilt's taste of soot
on my tongue, but no clue
to the words beforewards—
as if I'd deep-sixed my
dossier of *sorry*'s; so all
I jotted down was shame's
gist, stinging like rope burn;
plus leaf-rust, and a mad
boy's dash down the path
into woods we called The Glen.

My doctors can't give it a name,
Melissa said in our next-
to-last Keats Independent
Study. Tuesdays brought
a bluer pall to her forehead;
pain, as if her heart, wrapped
in tissue, had caught fire;
and wit soulful as this—
waiting for the damned
morphine to take feels like
waiting for Italian trains.

Justin tended toward wordless
quips. Once he pressed

a walnut in my palm. For luck?
Eighty-one, author of four
Lives, he didn't say. Top down
axial scans of the brain
resemble a pecan sliced
along the seam. Justin's gift
sits on my desk. The nutmeat
keeps for years so long
as it's left unshelled.

Tinnitus Song

Like a tiny dentist drilling, if dentists drilled
all day, and woke you, drilling still, at dawn.
Behind the drill, a cloudy hum, assuming

clouds hum. No remedies. Strategies only.
Buy white noise—wind through woodlands,
ocean-slur of surf—at Brookstone. Against

all reason turn Metallica *up*. The greater
the din the lesser the drone. After these,
what's left but hearing your body repine

chronically about its breakdown? Memory
served as therapy once, remember? Mother's
index finger made her moist rim of crystal

sing. In Mozart's mind, that whine became
Rondo for Glass Harmonica. But this needling
sticks in the groove of *Psycho*'s soundtrack:

mind turned brain; brain, skull. Thinking
back to its root—*tinnire,* to ring—is too self-
evident to distract. So you're stranded, once

again, with literature. *People frying fish: fry,
fry, fry all day,* cried Hardy, laureate of futility.
Or you're stuck in the echo chamber of cliché

amplified from facts so odd, who wouldn't give
them a try? Stick out your tongue, it's louder;
grit your teeth, it goes quieter. Grin and bear it.

Neoplatonic

Giordano Bruno came to me out of the flames when I should have been loading the dishwasher. Crusted egg, nubs of hamburger the prickly consistency of owl pellets. So much for the Theater of Memory.

But some magicians still make a good living. The top ten never manipulate balloons, fewer than you might think employ sequined assistants, and only the chuckleheads try to repeat what the thunder says. Once, a witch cleaned out my garage with the twitch of her eyebrow: my kind of reality inside reality. Three defunct leaf blowers! Of my many nonfunctional book lights, one resembles a hammerhead shark; another, both the lamp and jaws of a lantern fish. I'm looking out the window as more snow snows on snow, Nature's range of diction dispiritingly impoverished. *Give. Sympathize. Control. Alt. Delete.* Some say Bruno's last words were "Bless those that curse you." To me, however, he'll always be repeating, *Please help me with this ladder.*

Afterwards, the martyred Hermeticist turned his eyes away from me, as he always did when shown a crucifix.

Envy

Elizabeth I and Robert Devereux, Earl of Essex

Because he beheld her face
without the paste of white
lead and vinegar her ladies
administered as makeup
a concoction which in time
so chewed up her poxy skin
he's rumored to have said
too loud to a fellow courtier
facing her one faces the moon
she had him beheaded or so
the legend goes though some
say everyday treason
did him in and anyway
this poem is entitled
"Envy" not "Vanity"
oh my illustrious friends
I want to kill or become
standing there between me
and the lip of the sea

Two Poems in Memory of Wayne Brown

1

In Jamaica, if you live in the mountains, the slim, hairpin turns are relentless as Jehovah's Witnesses. You honk so much the mechanic replaces your car's horn along with its brakes. Everywhere, people smell the sea in the air. Not the ocean, the sea. They keep watch on the horizon, since it might be listening.

In Jamaica, it's good to write good poems, better to be a good poet. So thought my dear dead friend, Wayne—whose name doesn't mean "invisible giant" but does to me; whom I loved but couldn't tell I loved. He wouldn't hear of it. He'd rather sail. A thermos of rum and coke in one hand—*Is there anything more sacred than a child reading a book?*—in the other, his cap he'll set on my young son's head, whose name all afternoon will be First Mate.

2

I'm wan as a hand-worn hammer haft.
Every synapse is a snuffed wick. God,
did you leave a tooth under the pillow
of my keen brain this unsunny Sunday?
Time to check it out or Meet the Press.
Wayne insisted mankind use *until* or *till*,
but never *'til*. His final email ordered me
to live lucky. What was with that? Now
my heart's articulate with a mist the wet

grass expresses. Today I'll almost certainly
forget, except that it went defunct, like
this thought; no, that thought; no, this.
Oh shit, all I want is to construct
a frame for a house with that hammer;
or fire up something akin to darkness
with that wick—once I find a match.
Hello, you world determined to accept
not one pipette of light. To Wayne
I owe this apology for poetry: "arms
in turn around each dead, loved thing—
the gesture may be fruitless, but is made."

Justice

While corks popped, I led you up
through flickers, then swells, of applause.
Your lectern was a cairn of books, mine
risen from the base of yours.

You bowed. *Not unlike,* I thought, *that bum*
rummaging through trash near the hotel vestibule.
"*Vestibule,* in a poem," you said, "undoes
everything I taught you. Still, keep *trash.*"

Peering out, you winced, as when you'd tear
your glasses off and hold
our mimeo-blue bones up to the light.
Once, I swear, I saw you sniff.

"Now, now, if ever, love opening your eyes,"
you began, the line not yours but Weldon Kees—
yet done such justice, everyone
longed to be you being him … except me,

sorry. I'm keeping *vestibule,*
glad you liked *trash.* Though I can't defend the bum,
he stays. Afterwards, we allowed
one hug, as we'd never done

in a world where acids yellow
the signatures of your perfect-bound
debut, shelved between József and Juvenal.
The heat of that hug; the Bentons we shared; our smoke.

Bohemia Lies by the Sea

Thou art perfect, then, our ship hath touched upon
The deserts of Bohemia?
　　　　—A Winter's Tale

If the houses here are green, I'll step into a house.
If the bridges can't hold up, I'll walk on firm ground.
If every age loses its labors of love, I give up mine here.
If I'm not the one, someone is, and worth what I'm worth.

If a word limits me now, let it limit me then.
If Bohemia lies by the sea, I'll believe in the sea.
And if I believe in the sea, I can hope to see land.
If I am the one, anyone is, and worth what I'm worth.

I don't want anything else. Let me go underground,
meaning: under the sea, and rediscover Bohemia.
I'll wake up making peace with what I've ruined.
From the bottom is where I'll know I'm not lost.

Come here you Bohemians, sailors, harborside whores,
ships adrift. All you Illyrians, Venetians, and Veronese—
don't you want to be Bohemians? Don't you want to play
in the comedies that have us weeping laughter?

Don't you want to go wrong a hundred times,
as I went wrong, and couldn't withstand the trials?
In time, I withstood them—as Bohemia, one fine day,
withstood them, was pardoned, and now lies by water.

I'm still on the edge of a word and another country.
More and more I'm on the edge of everything.

I'm a citizen of Bohemia—an itinerant actor,
holding and held by nothing, allowed only to watch

the shore of my choice, from the questionable sea.

Notes

"Thought Experiment" owes a debt to Ian McEwan's novel, *Saturday*.

"I Want That" owes a debt to Laura Jensen's poem, "I Want Some."

The second section of "Three Versions of Mandelstam" is typically referred to as "The Stalin Epigram." All three sections derive from untitled poems.

"In Favor of Magical Thinking" refers to an incident in *War and Peace*, Volume Two, Part Four, Chapter 11.

In "Flight," the phrase "Enough! or Too Much!" is the last of the "Proverbs of Hell" from William Blake's *The Marriage of Heaven and Hell*.

The URL for the hyperlink in "Ours" is https://en.wikipedia. org/wiki/List_ of_ethnic_slurs#Z.

The first quotation attributed to Tolkien in "The Look" is a close approximation.

"An Invitation" and "Drink" adapt incidents and characters from two "microscripts" by Robert Walser, in *Robert Walser: Microscripts*, translated by Susan Bernofsky (New Directions, 2012).

The title to "The Benevolence of the Butcher" comes from a passage in Adam Smith's *An Inquiry into the Nature & Causes of the Wealth of Nations:* "It is not from the benevolence of the butcher, the brewer, or the baker that we expect our dinner, but from their regard to their own self-interest."

"En Route" adapts Eugenio Montale's poem, "Verso Vienna."

In "Devotion Street," the quoted line is from Rex Warner's translation of "A Word for Summer," by George Seferis.

"Tinnitus Song" makes use of some facts from Jerome Groopman's article, "That Buzzing Sound" (*The New Yorker*, February 9, 2009).

The lines quoted in Part Two of "Two Poems in Memory of Wayne Brown" come from his poem, "The Witness."

"Justice" is in memory of Donald Justice. The line attributed to Weldon Kees comes from Kees's poem, "A Late History."

"Bohemia Lies by the Sea" adapts Ingeborg Bachmann's poem, "Böhmen liegt am Meer."

Acknowledgements

Thanks to the editors of the following periodicals and anthologies, in which some of these poems, or earlier versions of them, originally appeared:

AGNI: Neoplatonic, Part 2 of Three Versions of Mandelstam

The American Journal of Poetry: American Freedom

The Antioch Review: Bohemia Lies by the Sea

The Autumn House Anthology of Contemporary American Poets (second edition): The Benevolence of the Butcher, Sketches at the Hayden Rec Center

Barrow Street: Devotion Street

Bellevue Literary Review: Frontier, Thought Experiment

Boulevard: Justice

Calabash: Dorado

The Carolina Quarterly: Without a Name for This

Crazyhorse: Self-Portrait with Insomnia, Rocks, and Fireflies

Cutbank Online: Part I of Two Poems in Memory of Wayne Brown, Written During a Depression

Field: En Route, I Want That

The Hampden-Sydney Poetry Review: Tinnitus Song

Lily Poetry Review: Argumentum ad Lapidem While on an Elliptical, In Dunedin

Little Star: Costco, In Favor of Magical Thinking

The Massachusetts Review: A Habit, South Belknap

Memorious: The Benevolence of the Butcher, Every Three Years

New England Review: After Tomaž Šalamun

New Ohio Review: Bad, The Game, Note to My First Wife

On the Seawall: Born to Be Wild, Listen

The Paris Review: Lackawanna

Passengers Journal: Time Out; Zuni Fetishes, Santa Fe

Perihelion: Chthonic

Ploughshares: Sketches at the Hayden Rec Center

Plume: A Burn So Bad It Requires Ice, Calling Back, Charity, Flight, The Look, Ours

Plume Anthology of Poetry 2014: The Great Chain of Being

Salamander: Elegy for My Family, Mentalese

Slate: Independence Day, Sewage Has Its Say

Sugar House Review: A Cosmography of Melancholy, Sunday Morning, Three Versions of Mandelstam, The World

Sycamore Review: Orphic

Tar River Poetry: Drink

upstreet: Part II of Two Poems in Memory of Wayne Brown

"Self-Portrait with Insomnia, Rocks, and Fireflies" appeared on *Poetry Daily* (January 27, 2007).

"Lackawanna" was printed as a broadside by Squircle Line Press.

"Dorado" was printed as part of the Arrowsmith Press Broadside Collection.

As ever, love and gratitude to Teresa Cader and Joyce Peseroff for what they see and won't let get by; to Joan Houlihan's eye for what's invisible, or ought to be; and to Thomas Swiss, poetry brother from way back, and now back again.

Thanks also to Michael Braverman, Jessie Crosby, and Sam Osherson.

About the Author

Listen is Steven Cramer's sixth poetry collection. His previous books of poetry are *The Eye that Desires to Look Upward* (Galileo Press, 1987), *The World Book* (Copper Beech Press, 1992), *Dialogue for the Left and Right Hand* (Lumen Editions/Brookline Books, 1997), *Goodbye to the Orchard* (Sarabande Books, 2004)—winner of the 2005 Sheila Motton Prize from the New England Poetry Club and named a 2005 Honor Book in Poetry by the Massachusetts Center for the Book—and *Clangings* (Sarabande Books, 2012). His poems and reviews have appeared in *The Atlantic Monthly, Field, Kenyon Review, The Nation, The New Republic, The Paris Review, Ploughshares, Poetry,* and other journals. His work is represented in anthologies such as *The Autumn House Anthology of Contemporary American Poetry* (Autumn House Press, 2005 and 2011), *The Book of Villanelles* (Knopf Everyman's Library Pocket Poets Series, 2012), and *The POETRY Anthology, 1912–2002* (Ivan R. Dee, 2002). He has also written essays for *Simply Lasting: Writers on Jane Kenyon* (Graywolf Press, 2005); *Touchstones: American Poets on a Favorite Poem* (Middlebury College Press, 1996); and *Until Everything Is Continuous Again: American Poets on the Recent Work of W. S. Merwin* (WordFarm, 2012). Recipient of two grants from the Massachusetts Cultural Council and a National Endowment for the Arts fellowship, he has taught literature and writing at Bennington College, Boston University, M.I.T., and Tufts University; and he founded and now teaches in the Low-Residency MFA Program in Creative Writing at Lesley University in Cambridge, Massachusetts.

www.ingramcontent.com/pod-product-compliance
Lightning Source LLC
Chambersburg PA
CBHW021342090426
42742CB00008B/710